HOUSE SPARROWS

EVERYWHERE

HOUSE SPARROWS
EVERYWHERE

by Caroline Arnold photographs by Richard R. Hewett

A Carolrhoda Nature Watch Book

Carolrhoda Books, Inc./Minneapolis

We would like to thank Sally and Eric Schreuder for allowing us to observe the birds in their back yard, and Lin and Jan Sircus for providing the opportunity to see sparrows in winter. We also thank Art, Jennifer, and Matthew Arnold for their assistance at many stages of this project.

LIBRARY OF CONGRESS CATALOGING-IN-PUBLICATION DATA

Arnold, Caroline.
    House sparrows everywhere / by Caroline Arnold ; photographs by
Richard R. Hewett.
        p.   cm.
    "A Carolrhoda nature watch book."
    Includes index.
    Summary: Describes the physical characteristics, habitat, and life
cycle of the house sparrow.
    ISBN 0-87614-696-5
    1. English sparrow—Juvenile literature. [1. English sparrow.
2. Sparrows.] I. Hewett, Richard, ill. II. Title.
QL696.P262A76 1992
598.8'73—dc20   91-26310
                                                   CIP
                                                    AC
Manufactured in the United States of America
1 2 3 4 5 6 7 8 9 10 01 00 99 98 97 96 95 94 93 92

Colorized black-and-white photographs of hand-reared house sparrows have been used on pages 26-29, 32-33

Additional photographs courtesy of: p. 10, Department of Entomology, University of Minnesota; p. 19 (bottom), 32, 33, Arthur Arnold; p. 28, 29, Caroline Arnold

Who is your nearest neighbor? Could it be a house sparrow? Almost everywhere people live, there are house sparrows. These sturdy and resourceful birds can be seen on busy street corners, at school yards, around shopping centers, and in people's yards. Their scientific name, *Passer domesticus,* comes from Latin words meaning "sparrow" and "belonging to the house." House sparrows have always lived near houses, farms, and city buildings. Watching them is one of the easiest ways to observe wild animal behavior in your own neighborhood.

The male sparrow (right) has white cheeks and a black bib. The female to his left does not have striking markings.

House sparrows are so common that most people do not look at them closely. The male has a handsome black bib on his chest, white cheeks, a rust eye-line, and a gray cap on his head. As with many other birds, the female is less colorfully marked. She has a tan eye stripe, a brown back, and a gray breast. Both are about 5 or 6 inches (12.7-15.2 cm) long.

The house sparrow, and its relatives in the weaver finch family, originally lived in Europe and Africa. When early settlers arrived in North America, they saw small brown birds that reminded them of the sparrows they had known in Europe, so they called the new birds sparrows too. They did not know that the American sparrows belong to a different group of birds. The

A male white-crowned sparrow

native North American sparrows such as the song sparrow, field sparrow, and white-crowned sparrow belong to another bird family, the Fringillids. House sparrows and weaver finches belong to the Ploceid family.

The only other member of the Ploceid group in North America is the European tree sparrow. It looks very much like the house sparrow except that the top of its head is rust rather than gray. The European tree sparrow lives chiefly in the area around St. Louis, Missouri. It is not a native bird—like the house sparrow, it was brought to the United States from Europe.

Before 1850, there was not a single house sparrow in the United States. Today there are millions. The story of how the house sparrow came to the United States and multiplied so successfully illustrates both the benefits and dangers of bringing wildlife to a new land. In nature, it is normal for plant and animal populations to change as conditions vary. When people interfere with this process, however, the delicate balance of nature can be upset. When a new kind of animal is introduced to an area, it takes over the **habitat**, or living places, of some native species as it searches for food and shelter. And without natural **predators,** animals that kill other animals for food, to keep the population from growing too fast, the new species may spread out of control.

Around 1850, insects were destroying the trees of many American cities. The worst pest was *Ennomos subsignaria,* commonly known as the inchworm or measuring worm. Millions of these worms chewed away the leaves of trees in early spring, leaving the branches almost bare. This was before the days of chemical pesticides, and no one could think of a way to get rid of the awful pests.

House sparrows were brought to the United States to get rid of this inchworm pest, Ennomos subsignaria.

10

The usefulness of sparrows in destroying harmful insects had been demonstrated in Prussia in the mid-1700s during the reign of Frederick the Great. Frederick was fond of eating cherries, and he was angered when he learned that sparrows had eaten some of his favorite fruit. So Frederick ordered that all sparrows be destroyed. In the next year, there were no sparrows to nibble at the cherries. But there were no cherries, either, because the insects had multiplied so greatly that they had devoured all the fruit. Frederick, now wiser, ordered that the sparrows be allowed back so they could eat the insects that were destroying the cherries. Some of the sparrows returned, but it took many years before they were completely reestablished.

In the United States, the inchworm did some of its worst damage in the New York City area. Nicholas Pike, who was the director of the Brooklyn Institute (now the Brooklyn Museum) in New York, knew that although adult house sparrows normally eat seeds, they feed insects and grubs to their babies during the nesting season. He thought that if he could bring some house sparrows to the United States, they might build nests and feed inchworms to their babies.

This house sparrow nest is well hidden by leaves.

A female house sparrow has collected food for her young.

In the fall of 1850, eight pairs of house sparrows were brought from England to the United States. They were released in the spring of 1851. More birds came in the fall of 1852. Some were released on the way into New York Harbor, and the rest were let go near the Brooklyn Institute in the spring of 1853. These house sparrows did well in their new home. They built nests and laid eggs. They fed their young thousands of inchworms and other insects. Nicholas Pike was proved right. The sparrows did help to get rid of the destructive inchworms.

Between 1854 and 1881, more house sparrows were brought from Europe and released in many other cities. Everybody called them "English" sparrows because many of them had come from England.

By 1900, house sparrows had spread throughout the United States. The rapid increase in the number of sparrows in the United States between 1850 and 1900 was linked to the growth in the human population during that time. As cities expanded and people spread over the country, there was also an increase in the number of horses. Horses were needed both for work and for transportation, and everywhere there were horses, there was grain. The sparrows lived on spilled grain from the horses' nose bags and feed troughs. Sparrows are still a common sight around horse stables. After 1900, when cars began to replace horses, the sparrow population declined—sparrows cannot eat spilled gasoline. Today, there are fewer sparrows than there were just before the invention of the automobile. Still, house sparrows are our most common bird.

The house sparrows did a great service when they got rid of the inchworms. However, the people who were so happy to see the inchworm destroyed were dismayed a few years later to discover a new insect pest—a small spiny-haired caterpillar. With the inchworm gone, these new caterpillars found plenty of food and multiplied quickly. People hoped the house sparrows would eat these caterpillars as well. But the sparrows did not like the bitter-tasting spiny-haired caterpillars.

Within a few years, after the house sparrows had become established, people began to regard the birds themselves as pests and wanted to get rid of them. But it was too late. There were too many house sparrows, and they had spread over too wide an area. Today, scientists are extremely careful about importing any new kind of plant or animal because it is difficult to predict how it might upset the balance of nature.

Farmers dislike house sparrows because large flocks of the birds sometimes eat their grain. They forget that the sparrows help them too. When sparrows are gathering food to feed their young, they destroy many insect pests that otherwise might eat the farmers' grain. Some of the harmful insects that sparrows feed to their chicks are Japanese beetles, aphids, cutworms, army worms, and locusts.

Even in cities, people often feel that large flocks of sparrows are a nuisance. Because sparrows are not brightly colored and do not have a beautiful song, many people do not find them attractive. Also, many bird lovers dislike house sparrows because they have taken over the nesting sites of native birds and have forced them to leave.

At dusk, sparrows look for ledges or branches where they can **roost**, or perch, for the night. When many sparrows roost together in trees or on buildings, they can be noisy and their droppings are messy. Sparrows can also be a problem at outdoor restaurants when they hop onto tables and grab bits of food— sometimes right from a customer's plate. To discourage sparrows and other birds, some restaurant owners put sharp edges on their roofs so birds have nowhere to perch. They may also put up statues of large predatory birds, such as owls, to scare away the small sparrows.

Another reason that house sparrows spread across the United States so rapidly is that they are extremely **adaptable**. House sparrows can live where it is cold or hot. They can find food even in crowded cities, and they will build their nests almost anywhere.

Sparrows do not migrate in winter and are one of the few birds that you can watch year-round. Even in very cold climates, sparrows can survive. House sparrows that live in cold climates have more feathers to keep them warm than those that live in the tropics. Their feathers are also slightly darker, which helps them absorb heat from the sun more easily. House sparrows have been known to live as far north as the Arctic Circle and as far south as Campbell Island, which is 400 miles (644 km) south of New Zealand. House sparrows live on every continent of the world except Antarctica.

Singing is one of the first outward signs that birds are ready to breed. With sparrows, as with many birds, only the male bird sings. His cheerful "chirrup, chirrup" attracts females and also tells other birds to stay away from his territory. Both males and females make another short, chirping sound, which is their call. Sparrows use these chirping calls to communicate with each other and to sound an alarm when danger is near.

During the late winter, changes take place inside sparrows' bodies, causing the production of chemical substances called **hormones**. In spring, as the days grow longer and the nights shorter, hormone levels increase. When hormones are at the right levels, sparrows are ready to start breeding.

A male sparrow courts a female by hopping in front of her with his head raised and wings outstretched. If she is interested, she may respond by pecking him. Often, two males compete for the same female, and this may lead to a fight or a chase. After the courtship period, a male and female become a pair, and together they search for a good place to build a nest. Once paired, a male and female sparrow usually stay together for life, often using the same nest site over and over.

At first, the male sits on top of a possible nest site and sings to attract his mate. The two birds inspect the site, and if it is suitable, they begin to build their nest there.

A good choice for a nest site is one that is cozy and well protected from the sun, wind, and rain. Sometimes, house sparrows choose natural nest sites, such as in trees or dense ivy, but just as often they use nest sites made by people. Many cities have unknowingly built thousands of nest sites for house sparrows. The hollow cross poles of traffic lights make perfect nest boxes for sparrows. Hollow street signs also are good nest boxes. Ledges under the eaves of buildings and at many railway station platforms are other favorite nesting places for sparrows. Sometimes, sparrows take over other birds' nests too.

Usually a sparrow nest is well hidden, but sometimes a telltale piece of loose nesting material lets you know that there is a nest inside. If you watch the birds in your neighborhood closely, you will probably discover several nests.

This house sparrow has found a good place to build a nest.

24

Dried grass, bits of string, and paper are the usual nesting materials for sparrows. The birds arrange them loosely and rather untidily inside the nest site. If the nest site does not provide a cover for the nest, the sparrows will weave one. Then the center of the nest is lined with soft grass and feathers.

Nests should be safe from animals such as cats and snakes, and have a small enough entrance so that larger birds such as bluejays and hawks cannot enter. These predators could destroy the nest and eat the eggs or young birds.

Sparrows have often been noted for their bravery. Watch how they behave around other kinds of birds and animals. If a cat approaches a sparrow nest, the parent sparrows will fly at it and seem to scold it. This is called **mobbing** and is done by many birds to annoy and distract a predator. Animals cannot make surprise attacks if they are being bothered in this way.

After the nest is finished, the sparrows mate and the female lays her eggs. When sparrows mate, the eggs inside the female's body become **fertilized**. If an egg is not fertilized, it will not develop and hatch. The female sparrow lays one egg a day for a period of four to six days. Each egg is about ¾ of an inch (2 cm) long and has a bluish-gray background with dark spots.

After the third egg is laid, the sparrows **incubate** the eggs by sitting on them to keep them warm and moist. During incubation, one of the parent birds stays on the nest all the time except for short periods when it leaves to look for food. Although parent birds take turns incubating the eggs, the female does the greater share, and she is the one who stays in the nest at night. Her dull coloring makes her hard to see in and around the nest. As soon as the eggs hatch, the male helps to feed the young birds.

The eggs are incubated for 12 to 15 days. Each day, the baby birds grow inside the eggs, and on the 15th day after the first egg was laid, they are ready to hatch. Even though the eggs are laid on different days, they hatch at about the same time because they are all incubated for about the same length of time. The first three eggs hatch first, and the rest hatch a day or two after that.

A baby bird is called a chick. When a sparrow chick is ready to hatch, it pushes against the inside of the shell with its **egg tooth**, a tiny, sharp point at the end of its beak. The egg tooth is not really a tooth and falls off soon after the bird is hatched.

At first, the chick uses its egg tooth to make a slit in the large end of the egg. As the chick rotates inside the shell, the slit forms a circle and the eggshell breaks in half. Now the sparrow chick can pop

out its head. Then, as the bird moves, the rest of the shell slowly breaks away.

A newly hatched sparrow chick weighs about ¹⁄₁₀ of an ounce (2.5 g) and is less than 1½ inches (4 cm) long. It is blind, featherless, and cannot walk or fly. The only thing it can do is open its mouth for food.

All birds are classified into two groups according to the development of the newly hatched chicks. Those whose chicks are completely helpless when they are hatched are called **altricial** birds. Like all songbirds, house sparrows are altricial. Chicks who are able to peck for food as soon as they are hatched are called **precocial** birds. Chickens, ducks, and geese are typical precocial birds— their chicks can see and walk, and are covered with downy feathers at the time of hatching.

House sparrow parents feed their chicks soft foods such as insects, grubs, or worms. They work hard to bring food to their young, making as many as 300 trips a day to the nest with food. The food provides energy for the babies to keep warm, to move, and to grow.

When a sparrow chick notices that a parent has entered the nest, it cheeps to communicate that it is hungry. This noise and the bright yellow edges of the young sparrow's mouth help the parents to locate it in the darkness of the nest.

When a sparrow is five days old, its eyes are open and it can see. When it's being fed, the baby bird sees its parents and learns to recognize them—a process called **imprinting**. As the young bird grows older, it learns to recognize the sparrow song and call as well.

When a bird eats, it swallows its food and stores it in a pouch on its neck called a **crop**. We do not usually see the crops of adult birds because they are covered with feathers. In a young sparrow that does not yet have all its feathers, you can see its full crop bulging with food.

A baby sparrow's first feathers begin to appear on the fourth day of life. They look like tiny black sticks because the soft parts are hidden by a hard cover, called a sheath. When a sparrow is eight or nine days old, the protective sheaths begin to wear off, making the soft feathers at the ends look like tiny paintbrushes. Gradually, the whole feather emerges. Soft down feathers lie close to the body and keep the sparrow chick warm. Rows of smooth contour feathers cover the body and protect it. Long, strong flight feathers grow on the wings and on the tail.

Above: *Each feather of this seven-day-old sparrow is covered by a hard sheath.*

Left: *You can see the full crop on the neck of this nine-day-old sparrow. Notice the soft feathers poking through their sheaths.*

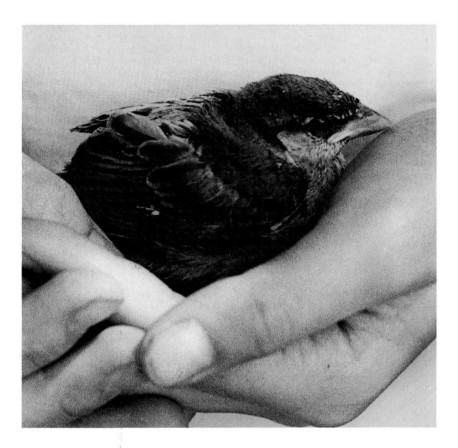

This two-week-old sparrow is ready to fledge.

The sparrow needs feathers to keep warm and to fly. You will notice that even full-grown sparrows are not particularly graceful fliers. Instead of swooping and gliding as some birds do, sparrows tend to flutter. The name "sparrow" comes from the Old German word "sparo," which means "flutterer."

When a sparrow chick is 14 to 17 days old, it is fully feathered and weighs slightly less than an ounce (25 g). It is ready to leave the nest. When a baby bird leaves its nest, we say that it has **fledged**. After fledging, it will never return to its nest. A fledgling bird is able to fly even though it has never flown before. At first it can fly only short distances, but with practice its wings become stronger.

Every spring, people find baby birds that seem to have fallen out of nests. Usually, these are fledgling birds. Even when the fledglings are out of sight, the parents know where to find them because they recognize the fledglings' cheeps.

The sparrow parents continue to feed their young for two or three weeks after they have fledged. When a young bird is hungry, it begs from its parents by opening its mouth wide and cheeping. At the same time, it rapidly flutters its wings. As the fledglings get older, the parents teach them to find their own food. By the time the young birds are about four weeks old, they can take care of themselves.

Male and female house sparrows look alike when they are in the nest and when they first fledge. As they grow older, though, males show the beginnings of black bibs. Males also begin to sing the typical house sparrow song. Those birds that do not sing or develop black bibs are females.

Adult sparrows eat mainly seeds and some insects, although they are not fussy and will eat whatever they can find. They are good scavengers and compete with bigger birds such as pigeons and starlings for scraps of food. If you put up a bird feeder, you will probably find that many of your guests will be house sparrows.

You may also see birds eating gravel or sand. Birds do not have teeth to chew their food. The sand mixes with their food in a part of their body called the **gizzard** and helps to grind the food into smaller pieces. The gizzard is located just beyond the stomach. Together, a bird's stomach and gizzard digests its food.

Like all animals, house sparrows need water to live. They find water in puddles, drinking fountains, streams, and sometimes under sprinklers.

The nesting season for house sparrows begins in spring and ends in the middle of summer. Each set of eggs is called a **clutch**, and it takes about one month for a pair of house sparrows to raise one clutch. During the nesting season, a pair of house sparrows may raise two or more clutches. They may use the same nest over and over, or they may build a new nest for each clutch.

Between late August and the end of October, sparrows lose their feathers and grow new ones. This is called **molt-ing**. A few feathers fall out at a time as new ones grow in, and gradually all the feathers are replaced. In cold climates, sparrows grow extra feathers to keep warm in the winter.

The new feathers come in with a gray fuzz on the tips so that sparrows in the fall do not seem to be as brightly colored as those you see in the spring. As spring approaches, the gray fuzz wears off and reveals the brighter coloring underneath.

Sparrows keep their feathers clean and smooth by **preening**. One by one, each feather is pulled through the bill to remove dirt and to realign any parts that may be out of order. Like most birds, sparrows have an oil gland at the base of the tail. Preening helps spread a thin layer of this oil over the feathers to make them resistant to water.

House sparrows also like to take baths in mud, dust, and water. Although sand and dust baths seem to be unlikely ways to keep clean, sparrows find them useful to remove lice and other tiny insects that sometimes live on their skin or feathers.

41

In late summer and through the fall and winter, house sparrows gather together in large flocks of dozens or even hundreds of birds. During the day, they look for food together, and at night they roost in trees or on buildings. They stay in their flocks until spring. Then the large groups break up, and the birds form pairs and begin the new breeding season. The young birds hatched during the previous summer will then be ready to mate and build their own nests.

You can learn a lot about house sparrows by watching them. If you have a bird feeder in your yard, you can watch sparrows at home. You can also watch sparrows in many public places—in parks, at school yards, in parking lots, or on street corners.

Whether we like it or not, the house sparrow is here to stay. House sparrows live successfully in North America because they can survive in many climates and conditions. They are sturdy and resourceful birds, able to adapt to new situations. Unlike many other kinds of birds, house sparrows have been able to coexist with people, and in fact have thrived near them. House sparrows are our most common bird. They may be your nearest neighbor.

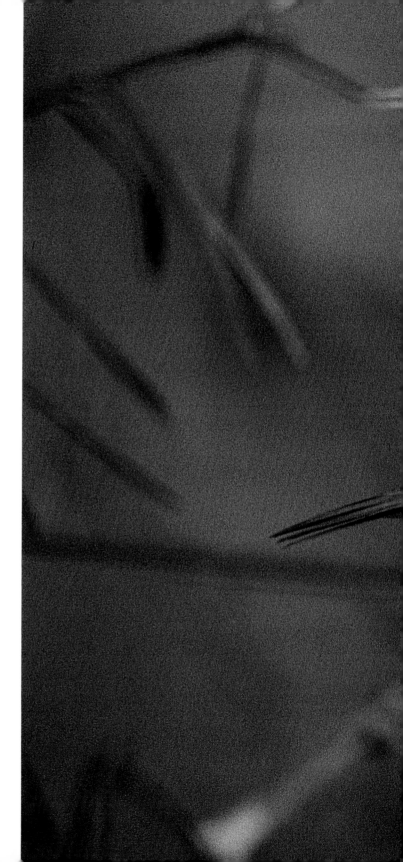

GLOSSARY

adaptable: able to adjust to varying conditions

altricial: being immature, helpless, and in need of care at the time of hatching. *Compare with precocial.*

clutch: a set of eggs that are incubated together

crop: a pouch for storing food, which is located on the neck of some birds

egg tooth: a tiny, sharp knob on a young bird's beak that is used to break out of the egg shell. After hatching, this special "tooth" falls off.

fertilize: to unite a male and a female reproductive cell, so that new life can develop

fledged: flown from the nest to begin an independent life

gizzard: an enlargement near the stomach of a bird that has tough, muscular walls used for grinding food

habitat: the area in which an animal normally lives

hormones: chemicals produced in an animal's body, which regulate various bodily functions and activities

imprinting: the process of a newborn animal learning to identify its parents

incubate: to sit on eggs, keeping them warm and moist so chicks will develop and hatch

mobbing: swooping down and annoying a potential predator

molting: shedding feathers periodically

precocial: able to walk and find food right after hatching. *Compare with altricial.*

predators: animals that kill and eat other animals

preening: cleaning and smoothing feathers with the bill

roost: to rest or sleep

INDEX

ABOUT THE AUTHOR

Caroline Arnold is the author of numerous widely acclaimed books for young readers, including the Carolrhoda Nature Watch titles *Saving the Peregrine Falcon, A Walk on the Great Barrier Reef, Tule Elk,* and *Ostriches and Other Flightless Birds.* Ms. Arnold lives in Los Angeles with her husband and their two children.

ABOUT THE PHOTOGRAPHER

Richard R. Hewett graduated from the Art Center School of Design, in California, with a major in photojournalism. He has illustrated more than 30 children's books and collaborated with Caroline Arnold on the Carolrhoda Nature Watch titles *Saving the Peregrine Falcon, Tule Elk,* and *Ostriches and Other Flightless Birds.* Mr. Hewett lives in Los Angeles with his wife.